Flatten Your Wheat Belly

Easy and Delicious Wheat Free Beginners Recipes to Lose Your Belly Fat and Feel Great

Printed in the United States of America.
First Printing, 2013

Table of Contents

iv

Introduction

In 2011, American cardiologist William R. Davis published a book describing his stance against wheat as a dietary staple – this book was called *Wheat Belly*. The book became a bestseller within one month of its publication and it has been featured on talk shows, websites and blogs for the past several years.

Thousands, perhaps millions, have been affected by the information in this book and have begun to live wheat-free lives. But what is it about this book that is so compelling?

Throughout his book, Dr. Davis explains the many dangers that wheat consumption can have for our bodies and for our health. Not only is wheat a common trigger for food allergies, but it is

The Wheat Belly Cookbook

something your body can actually become addicted to. Furthermore, Davis suggests that overconsumption of wheat is responsible for rising obesity rates in Western countries. The secret to healthy weight loss, Davis says, is to eliminate wheat from your diet.

In this book you will learn the basics about how wheat affects your diet and your body, as well as the dangers it poses. You will learn how to live without wheat, and come to understand the benefits you can expect from such a change. To cap it all off, you will receive 100 delicious wheat-free recipes to get you started in your new wheat-free lifestyle.

What is the Wheat Belly Diet?

The wheat belly diet is simply a wheat-free diet designed to remove and reverse the ill effects of wheat consumption on your body and on your health. Before you learn the details about how to follow the wheat belly diet, you need to understand WHY it is important. What does wheat do to your body and how does it happen? What does science have to say about living a wheat-free life?

You will learn the answers to all of these questions and more in this chapter.

Why Wheat is Addictive

For many people, wheat is a dietary staple and something they couldn't dream of living without. The truth goes much deeper than that, however – wheat can actually have an addictive effect on your body. The human body operates through an opioidergic system – the body has natural ways of issuing rewards in order to modulate behavior.

For example, exercise often produces a rush of endorphins which, for many people, is an encouragement to exercise more often. In reality, endogenous opioids produced by the body during times of stress (such as exercise) interact with opiate receptors in the brain to produce endorphins.

The consumption of wheat has a similar effect on your body in that it "rewards" you for eating it. Certain substances, like opiate drugs contain exorphins, or exogenous opioid peptides, which trigger cravings and addiction. Exorphins aren't just found in drugs, however – they are also found in certain foods including wheat and gluten.

Flatten Your Wheat Belly

When you ingest wheat, your body begins to produce enzymes to break it down (digestion). During this process, the components of wheat are broken down and absorbed into the bloodstream – this process releases the exorphins which make you feel satisfied. This feeling of satisfaction leads to cravings for the food and an addict-like response.

How Wheat Affects Your Body

As part of recent health trends, many people have made the switch from regular pasta and bread to whole wheat and whole grain alternatives. The wheat belly diet, however, suggests that wheat is bad in any form. Whether processed, bleached or whole grain, wheat has a negative effect on the body. Dr. Davis suggests that wheat is to blame for central obesity – the stubborn fat located within the abdomen, surrounding the internal organs.

Excess abdominal fat has been linked to numerous chronic diseases including diabetes, cancer and cardiovascular disease. Consumption of wheat and other high-carb foods contributes to the accumulation of this fat.

The Science of the Wheat Belly Diet

There is more to the wheat belly diet than simply breaking the addiction cycle of wheat consumption. In recent years, genetic modification has become an important part of the food industry and wheat has been greatly affected.

Strains of wheat have been crossbred and hybridized to increase crop yield and to make the plants resistant to insects and environmental changes. These modifications change not only the genetic code of wheat, but also the way our bodies and our immune systems react when we eat it. This has led to an increase in wheat-related allergies and a host of other serious problems.

Flatten Your Wheat Belly

Another important aspect of the wheat belly diet is the glycemic index. The glycemic index is a scale used to rate foods based on their ability to change blood sugar levels in the body. Foods with a low glycemic index are generally absorbed slowly – foods like vegetables and fruits – so they do not have a sudden impact on blood sugar levels. High glycemic foods like pasta, bread and cereal, however, cause quick spikes in blood sugar which can be very dangerous for diabetics.

Studies have shown that low-glycemic diets, like the wheat belly diet, are beneficial for not just the health of diabetics but for anyone.

In 2012, a study was published in the *Journal of the National Cancer Institute* regarding the effects of carbohydrate intake on cancer patients. Over 1,000 patients were surveyed and it was found that those who had higher glycemic loads in their diet were almost twice as likely to experience a recurrence.

In June of 2012, *The Journal of the American Medical Association* published a study which revealed that low-glycemic diets helped to support healthy weight loss by regulating the metabolism.

Wheat's Destruction of Your Health

Common Ailments Associated with Wheat

If you pay any attention at all to health and fitness trends, or simply watch the news, you have probably heard about rising obesity rates and countless other diseases plaguing modern Western countries. Scientists agree that a large portion of these problems are due to the unhealthy eating habits of Americans and other Western cultures.

Wheat, as a staple of the modern Western diet, plays a big role in causing and exacerbating these problems. Obesity is not the only problem in which wheat plays a role. Some of the other ailments and conditions associated with wheat consumption include:

- Abdominal fat storage
- Type II diabetes
- Increased risk for cardiovascular disease
- Join pain and inflammation
- Acne and other skin problems
- Rheumatoid arthritis

· Decreased cognitive function
· Increased cancer risk
· Decreased insulin response
· Food allergies and intolerance

How Wheat Contributes to Health Problems

Wheat contributes to a number of negative health effects, not limited to the conditions listed above. You have already learned the basics regarding how wheat affects your appetite and cravings, as well as the ways it can affect fat storage and blood sugar levels.

One of the most common and most serious health problems associated with wheat consumption, that has not yet been discussed, is wheat allergies and intolerance. Food allergies – particularly those involving wheat – have become more prevalent in the past few decades and more people than ever are being diagnosed with celiac disease.

Celiac disease is actually an autoimmune disorder triggered by the consumption of gluten (a protein found in wheat, barley and rye) but it is closely associated to wheat allergies and intolerance. Both wheat allergies and wheat intolerance cause similar symptoms, but the severity and onset of the symptoms may vary.

For wheat intolerant individuals, for example, consuming a large amount of wheat might cause stomach pain, nausea, diarrhea or vomiting, and the symptoms often come on gradually. In the case of an allergy, however, these symptoms may be severe and typically come on quickly.

If you continue to consume wheat on a regular basis, your body will continue to experience damage. For individuals with celiac disease, the consumption of gluten triggers an immune response – the body produces antibodies to fight the gluten, which also end up attacking the tissues in the gut.

Repeated exposure to gluten causes intestinal damage, which can lead to the malabsorption of nutrients and a variety of other problems. If you are serious about reversing or avoiding the negative effects of wheat on your body, consider switching to a wheat-free lifestyle.

How to Live Without Wheat

For those experiencing the ill effects of wheat consumption, there is only one solution. There is no pill you can take or miracle remedy to stave off the effects – the only solution is to remove wheat from your diet. This is the premise of the wheat belly diet and it is the only way to break free from the grasp that unhealthy wheat has on your body and your health. In this chapter you will learn what life after wheat can be like, and some of the benefits you will experience following the wheat belly diet.

Life After Wheat

If you are like many people in modern Western countries, wheat-based foods are a staple in your diet. You may eat cereal or a bagel for breakfast, a sandwich for lunch and fried chicken for dinner. Wheat has nearly become its own food group and many people do not realize the risks. In reading this book and making the switch to a wheat-free diet, you are ahead of the game, but you should realize that the transition might be tricky.

Think back to the first chapter in which we discussed the addictive qualities of wheat. As you begin to eliminate wheat from your diet, you may experience increased cravings at first. After a few days, however, your body will get used to being wheat-free and you will begin to experience the benefits of a wheat-free diet.

Just take your time and cut down on the amount of wheat you consume slowly as you make the transition. In a matter of weeks you will begin to feel like an entirely new person – you may even experience drastic improvements after the first few days!

Advantages of Living Wheat-Free

The wheat belly diet has a number of potential advantages for anyone who switches to the diet. Some of these advantages and benefits may include:

- Reduced cravings and regulated appetite
- Increased weight loss results
- Lowered cholesterol levels
- Improved skin health, reduced acne
- Relief from the pain of arthritis
- Improved bone density

- Lowered risk for cancer, diabetes and heart disease
- Reduced inflammation
- Improved digestion/relief from indigestion
- Relief from joint pain
- Improved insulin response, fewer blood sugar spikes

Now that you understand the wheat belly diet and the benefits of living wheat-free, you should be ready to get started. In the next chapter you will receive 100 delicious wheat-free recipes to get you started in your wheat-free lifestyle!

100 Belly-Shrinking
Wheat-Free Recipes

Breakfast Recipes

Apple Cinnamon Muffins

Ingredients:

2 cups old-fashioned oats

¼ cup packed brown sugar

1 ½ tsp. ground cinnamon

1 tsp. baking powder

Pinch of salt

1 ½ cups skim milk

1 ripe apple, peeled and grated

¼ cup unsweetened applesauce

½ cup liquid egg whites

½ cup raisins

Directions:

1. Preheat the oven to 350°F and grease a cupcake pan with cooking spray.
2. Combine the oats, brown sugar, baking powder, cinnamon and salt in a mixing bowl and stir well.
3. In another bowl, whisk together the milk, applesauce and egg whites.
4. Whisk the liquid ingredients into the oat mixture then fold in the grated apple and raisins.
5. Spoon the batter into the prepared cupcake pan, filling each cup about 2/3 full.
6. Bake for 30 to 40 minutes until a knife inserted in the center comes out clean.
7. Cool in the pan for 5 minutes, then turn out onto a wire rack to cool completely.

Banana Nut Muffins

Ingredients:

2 cups ground almond meal
1 cup mashed banana
¼ cup honey
4 large eggs, whisked
1 tsp. ground cinnamon
1 tsp. white vinegar
½ tsp. baking soda
½ cup chopped pecans

Directions:

1. Preheat the oven to 350°F and line a muffin pan with paper liners.
2. Combine the dry ingredients in a mixing bowl and stir well.
3. In another bowl, beat together the honey, eggs and vinegar.
4. Add the dry ingredients and stir until smooth and well combined.
5. Fold in the mashed banana and chopped pecans.
6. Spoon the batter into the prepared pan and bake for 15 to 18 minutes until a knife inserted in the center comes out clean.
7. Cool for 5 minutes in the pan, then turn out to cool completely.

Green Onion Scrambled Eggs

Ingredients:

2 tsp. olive oil

4 large eggs

1 tbsp. skim milk

1 small shallot, diced

¼ cup sliced green onion

1 clove garlic, minced

Pinch salt and pepper

Directions:

1. Heat the olive oil in a skillet over medium-high heat.
2. Whisk together the eggs, milk, green onion, salt and pepper in a small bowl.
3. Add the shallot and garlic to the skillet and cook for 2 minutes.
4. Pour in the egg mixture and let cook for 1 minute.
5. Stir the egg mixture while cooking for an additional 4 to 6 minutes until the egg is cooked through.

The Wheat Belly Cookbook

Coconut Flour Blueberry Pancakes

Ingredients:

½ cup coconut flour
¼ cup unsweetened applesauce
3 large eggs, whisked
2 tbsp. skim milk
2 tbsp. canola oil
2 tbsp. maple syrup
½ tsp. baking soda
½ tsp. vanilla extract
1 cup fresh blueberries

Directions:

1. Preheat a nonstick griddle to 400°F.
2. Combine the coconut flour and baking soda in a bowl.
3. In another bowl, beat together the applesauce, eggs, milk, canola oil, maple syrup and vanilla extract.
4. Add the flour mixture to the wet ingredients and whisk until smooth.
5. Spoon the batter onto the griddle in heaping tablespoons and sprinkle each pancake with a handful of blueberries.
6. Let the batter cook until bubbles form on the surface then carefully flip the pancakes.
7. Cook for an additional 1 to 2 minutes until the underside is lightly browned.

8. Remove the pancakes to a plate and repeat with the remaining batter.

Minty Melon Fruit Salad

Ingredients:

2 cups chopped watermelon
1 cup chopped honeydew
1 cup chopped cantaloupe
1 cup seedless grapes, halved
¼ cup fresh mint leaves, chopped
1 tbsp. fresh lemon juice
1 tsp. honey

Directions:

1. Combine the fruit in a serving bowl and toss with the mint, lemon juice and honey.
2. Chill until ready to serve.

Tomato and Onion Omelet

Ingredients:

2 tsp. canola oil
2 large eggs
1 tbsp. skim milk
1 small plum tomato, chopped
¼ cup diced yellow onion
Salt and pepper to taste

Directions:

1. Heat 1 tsp. canola oil in a skillet over medium heat.
2. Add the tomato and onion and cook for 2 to 3 minutes until the tomato begins to soften.
3. Spoon the mixture into a bowl and set aside.
4. Heat the remaining canola oil in the skillet.
5. Whisk together the eggs, milk, salt and pepper then pour into the skillet.
6. Let the egg cook for 1 minute then swirl the pan to coat the sides.
7. Cook for 1 minute more then scrape down the sides using a spatula, letting the uncooked egg spread.
8. Let cook for 1 to 2 minutes more until the egg is almost set.
9. Spoon the tomato and onion mixture over half the omelet and fold the empty half over top.
10. Cook until the egg is set then transfer to a plate to serve.

Cinnamon Pumpkin Muffins

Ingredients:

2 cups ground almond meal

¾ cup pumpkin puree

¼ cup honey

4 large eggs, whisked

1 tsp. ground cinnamon

1 tsp. white vinegar

½ tsp. baking soda

Directions:

1. Preheat the oven to 350°F and line a muffin pan with paper liners.
2. Combine the dry ingredients in a mixing bowl and stir well.
3. In another bowl, beat together the honey, eggs and vinegar.
4. Add the dry ingredients to the wet mixture and stir until smooth and well combined.
5. Fold in the pumpkin puree.
6. Spoon the batter into the prepared pan and bake for 15 to 18 minutes until a knife inserted in the center comes out clean.
7. Cool for 5 minutes in the pan, then turn out to cool completely.

Chocolate Chip Pancakes

Ingredients:

½ cup coconut flour
¼ cup unsweetened applesauce
3 large eggs, whisked
2 tbsp. canola oil
2 tbsp. honey
½ tsp. baking soda
½ tsp. vanilla extract
1 cup mini chocolate chips

Directions:

1. Preheat a nonstick griddle to 400°F.
2. Combine the coconut flour and baking soda in a bowl.
3. In another bowl, beat together the applesauce, eggs, canola oil, honey and vanilla extract.
4. Add the flour mixture to the wet ingredients and whisk until smooth.
5. Spoon the batter onto the griddle in heaping tablespoons and sprinkle each pancake with chocolate chips.
6. Let the batter cook until bubbles form on the surface, then carefully flip the pancakes.
7. Cook for an additional 1 to 2 minutes until the underside is lightly browned.
8. Remove the pancakes to a plate and repeat with the remaining batter.

Ham and Cheese Frittata

Ingredients:

1 tbsp. canola oil
8 large eggs
1 clove garlic, minced
1 cup diced deli ham
½ cup shredded cheddar cheese
Salt and pepper to taste
2 tbsp. grated parmesan cheese

Directions:

1. Preheat the oven to 400°F.
2. Heat the canola oil in an oven-proof skillet over medium heat.
3. Add the garlic and cook for 1 minute.
4. Add the ham and cook for 1 minute more.
5. Whisk together the eggs, milk, salt and pepper then pour into the skillet.
6. Sprinkle the shredded cheddar cheese onto the egg.
7. Cook for 3 to 4 minutes until the edges begin to set up then transfer the skillet to the oven.
8. Bake the frittata for 10 minutes then remove from the oven and let it sit, covered, for 5 minutes.
9. Garnish with grated parmesan and slice to serve.

Mushroom Zucchini Omelet

Ingredients:

2 tsp. canola oil
2 large eggs
1 tbsp. skim milk
1 small shallot, diced
½ cup zucchini, chopped
½ cup chopped mushroom
Salt and pepper to taste

Directions:

1. Heat 1 tsp. canola oil in a skillet over medium heat.
2. Add the shallot, zucchini and mushroom then cook for 3 to 4 minutes until the zucchini begins to soften.
3. Spoon the mixture into a bowl and set aside.
4. Heat the remaining canola oil in the skillet.
5. Whisk together the eggs, milk, salt and pepper then pour into the skillet.
6. Let the egg cook for 1 minute then swirl the pan to coat the sides.
7. Cook for 1 minute more, then scrape down the sides using a spatula, letting the uncooked egg spread.
8. Let cook for 1 to 2 minutes more until the egg is almost set.
9. Spoon the mushroom and zucchini mixture over half the omelet and fold the empty half over top.
10. Cook until the egg is set then transfer to a plate to serve.

Blueberry Granola Parfait

Ingredients:

1 cup fresh blueberries
¾ cup plain nonfat Greek yogurt
½ cup gluten-free granola

Directions:

1. Spoon about ¼ cup blueberries into the bottom of two parfait glasses.
2. Top the berries with ¼ cup Greek yogurt and 1 tbsp. granola.
3. Create a second layer of blueberries and yogurt then top the parfaits with the remaining granola to serve.

Banana Walnut Pancakes

Ingredients:

½ cup mashed banana
¼ cup coconut flour
3 large eggs, whisked
2 tbsp. canola oil
2 tbsp. maple syrup
½ tsp. baking soda
½ tsp. vanilla extract
1 cup chopped walnuts

Directions:

1. Preheat a nonstick griddle to 400°F.
2. Combine the coconut flour and baking soda in a bowl.
3. In another bowl, beat together the eggs, canola oil, maple syrup and vanilla extract.
4. Add the flour mixture to the wet and whisk smooth.
5. Fold in the mashed banana.
6. Spoon the batter onto the griddle in heaping tablespoons and sprinkle each pancake with chopped walnuts.
7. Let the batter cook until bubbles form on the surface then carefully flip the pancakes.
8. Cook for an additional 1 to 2 minutes until the underside is lightly browned.
9. Remove the pancakes to a plate and repeat with the remaining batter.

<u>Lunch Recipes</u>

Lime Cilantro Grilled Shrimp

Ingredients:

1 lbs. raw shrimp, peeled and deveined
½ cup fresh cilantro leaves, chopped
2 tbsp. olive oil
2 tbsp. fresh lime juice
Salt and pepper to taste

Directions:

1. Rinse the shrimp well then pat dry.
2. Place the shrimp in a plastic bag with the cilantro and shake.
3. Add the olive oil, lime juice, salt and pepper and toss to coat.
4. Chill the shrimp for about 20 minutes.
5. Preheat a stove-top grill pan over medium-high heat and grease with cooking spray.
6. Use a pair of tongs to arrange the shrimp on the grill pan, cooking for 1 to 2 minutes on each side until cooked through.

The Wheat Belly Cookbook

Butternut Squash Soup

Ingredients:

2 tbsp. olive oil
1 tsp. minced garlic
1 medium yellow onion, chopped
1 stalk celery, chopped
1 carrot, chopped
4 cups butternut squash, cubed
4 cups chicken broth
½ tsp. dried thyme
½ tsp. dried oregano
Salt and pepper to taste

Directions:

1. Heat the olive oil in a stockpot over medium-high heat.
2. Add the garlic and cook for 1 minute.
3. Stir in the onion, celery and carrot and cook for 4 minutes more.
4. Add the remaining ingredients and bring to a boil.
5. Reduce heat and simmer for 25 to 30 minutes until the squash is tender.
6. Remove from heat and puree using an immersion blender.

Apple Pecan Chicken Salad

Ingredients:

2 boneless skinless chicken breasts, cooked
1 medium apple, cored and chopped
½ cup seedless grapes, halved
3 tbsp. finely chopped pecans
2 tbsp. olive oil mayonnaise
1 tbsp. sesame tahini
1 tbsp. fresh lemon juice
Salt and pepper to taste

Directions:

1. Shred the chicken by hand into a mixing bowl.
2. Add the apple, grapes and pecans and stir well.
3. Stir in the remaining ingredients and toss to coat.
4. Chill until ready to serve.

Honey Balsamic Chicken Lettuce Wraps

Ingredients:

2 boneless skinless chicken breasts, cooked
6 to 8 large leaves of Boston lettuce
2 green onions, sliced
1 medium carrot, grated
1 tbsp. olive oil
1 tbsp. honey
1 tsp. balsamic vinegar
Pinch salt and pepper

Directions:

1. Shred the cooked chicken by hand and place into a bowl.
2. Whisk together the olive oil, honey, balsamic vinegar, salt and pepper and pour it over the chicken.
3. Toss the chicken to coat with dressing.
4. Lay the lettuce leaves out on a plate and spoon the chicken evenly into the cups.
5. Top with green onion and grated carrot then wrap the lettuce leaves up to serve.

Cream of Cauliflower Soup

Ingredients:

1 lbs. chopped cauliflower florets

3 cups water

1 tbsp. olive oil

1 tsp. minced garlic

1 medium yellow onion, diced

¼ cup half-and-half

1 tsp. dried thyme

½ tsp. dried oregano

Salt and pepper to taste

Directions:

1. Bring the water to a boil in a stockpot then add the cauliflower.
2. Boil for 2 to 3 minutes then drain the cauliflower, reserving the water.
3. Heat the olive oil in a large saucepan over medium-high heat.
4. Add the garlic and cook for 1 minute.
5. Stir in the onions and cook for 5 minutes more.
6. Add the steamed cauliflower, reserved water, thyme and oregano – season with salt and pepper to taste.
7. Bring the soup to a boil then reduce heat and simmer for 20 minutes.
8. Remove from heat and puree the soup using an immersion blender.
9. Whisk in the half-and-half and serve hot.

The Wheat Belly Cookbook
Easy Fried Fish Sticks

Ingredients:

1 lbs. boneless cod fillets
1 large egg
½ cup ground almond meal
½ tsp. dried oregano
½ tsp. dried basil
Salt and pepper to taste
Cooking oil

Directions:

1. Rinse the fish in cool water and pat it dry.
2. Slice the fish into 1-inch strips and set aside.
3. Beat the egg in a shallow dish.
4. In another shallow dish, stir together the almond meal, oregano, basil, salt and pepper.
5. Dip the fish sticks in the egg then dredge in the almond flour mixture.
6. Heat about ½ inch of cooking oil in a heavy skillet over medium-high heat.
7. Add the fish sticks and fry for 2 to 3 minutes on each side until golden brown.
8. Place on paper towels to drain before serving.

White Bean Soup

Ingredients:

½ lbs. dry white cannellini beans
1 large yellow onion, chopped
2 tbsp. olive oil
1 tbsp. minced garlic
2 ½ cups organic chicken broth
4 cups water
1 tsp. dried rosemary
1 tsp. dried oregano
Salt and pepper to taste
2 cups chopped kale

Directions:

1. Place the beans in a stockpot and cover with 2 inches of water.
2. Bring the beans to a boil then remove from heat and let stand, uncovered, for about 1 hour.
3. Drain the beans and rinse them well.
4. Heat the oil in a stockpot over medium-high heat.
5. Add the garlic and cook 1 minute.
6. Stir in the onions and cook for about 5 minutes
7. Add the cooked beans, chicken broth, water and seasonings, then simmer for 45 minutes until the beans are tender.
8. Stir in the chopped kale and simmer for another 5 to 10 minutes until the kale is softened. Serve hot.

The Wheat Belly Cookbook
Pineapple Kale Salad

Ingredients:

4 cups chopped kale
1 cup chopped pineapple
1 carrot, grated
1 green onion, sliced
2 tbsp. fresh lemon juice
1 tbsp. canola oil
1 tsp. red wine vinegar
1 tsp. poppy seeds
Pinch salt and pepper

Directions:

1. Combine the kale, pineapple, carrot and green onion in a salad bowl.
2. Whisk together the remaining ingredients and pour over the salad.
3. Toss to coat and chill until ready to serve.

Avocado Tuna Salad on Lettuce

Ingredients:

2 (7 oz.) cans tuna in water
2 ripe avocados, pitted
1 tbsp. olive oil mayonnaise
½ small red onion, diced
2 stalks celery, finely diced
1 carrot, finely diced
1 clove garlic, minced
2 tbsp. fresh lemon juice
Salt and pepper to taste

Directions:

1. Drain the tuna and shred it with a fork into a bowl.
2. In a separate bowl, mash the avocado.
3. Stir the shredded tuna into the avocado with the remaining ingredients.
4. Chill for 1 hour then serve on a bed of lettuce.

The Wheat Belly Cookbook

Red Bean Chili

Ingredients:

2 lbs. lean ground turkey
2 (15 oz.) cans red kidney beans, drained
1 (14.5 oz.) can diced tomatoes
1 large yellow onion, diced
1 tbsp. minced garlic
1 cup organic beef broth
¼ cup chili powder
1 tbsp. ground cumin
1 tsp. unsweetened cocoa powder
1 tsp. salt
½ tsp. black pepper

Directions:

1. Heat the turkey in a deep skillet over medium-high heat.
2. Cook, stirring often, until browned – about 5 minutes.
3. Stir in the garlic and onion and cook for 3 to 5 minutes until the onions turn translucent.
4. Stir in the beef broth, chili powder, cumin, cocoa powder, tomatoes, salt and pepper.
5. Reduce the heat and simmer, covered, for 15 minutes.
6. Add the beans then simmer, uncovered, for another 10 minutes. Serve hot.

Spinach Salad with Bacon and Egg

Ingredients:

4 cups fresh baby spinach
2 hardboiled eggs, peeled and chopped
¼ cup thinly sliced red onion
3 slices uncooked bacon
1 tbsp. olive oil
1 tbsp. red wine vinegar
Pinch dry mustard powder

Directions:

1. Place the spinach and red onion in a salad bowl and toss to combine.
2. Chop the bacon and heat it in a skillet over medium-high heat.
3. Cook the bacon until crisp then remove it from the skillet with a slotted spoon onto a paper towel to drain.
4. Whisk the olive oil, red wine vinegar and mustard powder into the skillet.
5. Remove the dressing from the heat and let it cool slightly.
6. Top the salad with chopped egg and bacon then drizzle with warm dressing to serve.

The Wheat Belly Cookbook

Coconut Chicken Nuggets

Ingredients:

1 lbs. boneless skinless chicken
2 large eggs
½ cup unsweetened shredded coconut
¼ cup coconut flour
Salt and pepper to taste
Cooking oil

Directions:

1. Pound the chicken to about ½-inch thickness using a mallet.
2. Cut the chicken into 2-inch chunks and set them aside.
3. In a shallow bowl, beat the eggs.
4. In another shallow bowl, whisk together the coconut, coconut flour, salt and pepper.
5. Dip the chicken chunks in egg then dredge in the coconut mixture.
6. Heat about ½-inch cooking oil in a heavy skillet over medium-high heat.
7. Add the chicken nuggets and fry for 2 to 3 minutes on each side until golden brown.
8. Place on a paper towel to drain before serving.

Strawberry Pecan Salad

Ingredients:

4 cups chopped romaine lettuce
1 cup chopped strawberries
1 stalk celery, thinly sliced
¼ cup thinly sliced red onion
3 to 4 tbsp. finely chopped pecans

Directions:

1. Combine the romaine lettuce, celery and red onion in a salad bowl.
2. Toss well then sprinkle with strawberries and pecans.
3. Serve with your preferred dressing.

Cream of Mushroom Soup

Ingredients:

1 lbs. sliced mushrooms
1 tbsp. olive oil
2 tbsp. minced shallots
1 tbsp. minced garlic
2 cups organic chicken stock
1 ½ cups heavy cream
½ tsp. dried thyme
Salt and pepper to taste
1 tbsp. water
1 tsp. cornstarch

Directions:

1. Place the mushrooms in a food processor and pulse until finely chopped.
2. Heat the olive oil in a stockpot over medium heat.
3. Add the shallots and garlic and cook for 1 minutes.
4. Stir in the mushrooms and cook for 10 minutes, stirring, until most of the liquid evaporates.
5. Add the chicken stock, cream, thyme, salt and pepper and stir well.
6. Bring to a boil then reduce heat and simmer for 20 minutes.
7. Whisk together the water and cornstarch then whisk it into the soup.
8. Simmer for 5 minutes to thicken then serve hot.

Dinner Recipes

The Wheat Belly Cookbook

Cracked Pepper Roasted Pork Loin

Ingredients:

2 lbs. boneless pork loin
1 tbsp. olive oil
1 tsp. fresh cracked pepper
Salt to taste

Directions:

1. Preheat oven to 350°F.
2. Rub the skin of the pork with olive oil then sprinkle with cracked pepper and salt.
3. Place the pork loin upside down on a roasting pan and roast for 30 minutes.
4. Turn the pork loin fat-side up and roast for another 20 to 25 minutes until the internal temperature reaches 155°F.
5. Remove the pork loin to a cutting board and cover with foil.
6. Let stand for 10 minutes before carving.

Shrimp and Garlic "Pasta"

Ingredients:

¾ lbs. raw shrimp, peeled and deveined
1 tbsp. olive oil
1 tsp. minced garlic
1 medium yellow onion, diced
2 large zucchini
1 tbsp. fresh lemon juice
¼ tsp. dried oregano
¼ tsp. dried thyme
Salt and pepper to taste

Directions:

1. Rinse the shrimp well and pat dry with paper towels.
2. Heat the olive oil in a skillet over medium heat.
3. Add the garlic and cook for 1 minute.
4. Stir in the onion and cook for 4 to 5 minutes until translucent.
5. Add the zucchini and toss with the lemon juice, oregano and thyme.
6. Cook for 2 minutes.
7. Add the shrimp and stir well then cover.
8. Cook for 2 to 3 minutes until the shrimp is cooked through.
9. Season with salt and pepper to taste. Serve hot.

Cranberry Chicken Legs

Ingredients:

4 lbs. chicken leg quarters
1 (14 oz.) can cranberry sauce
1 cup honey barbecue sauce
1 medium yellow onion, chopped
Salt and pepper to taste

Directions:

1. Arrange the chicken in a 3-quart slow cooker and sprinkled with onions.
2. Whisk together the remaining ingredients and pour over the chicken.
3. Cover the slow cooker and cook on low heat for 5 to 6 hours until the chicken is cooked through.
4. Serve hot over a bed of steamed rice.

Lemon Halibut with Mango Salsa

Ingredients:

1 lbs. fresh halibut fillets, boneless
1 tbsp. olive oil
1 fresh lemon, sliced
Salt and pepper to taste

1 ripe mango, pitted and chopped
1 small tomato, diced
¼ cup fresh chopped cilantro
2 tbsp. minced red onion
1 tbsp. fresh lemon juice

Directions:

1. Preheat the oven to 350°F and line a baking sheet with foil.
2. Rinse the fish and pat dry with paper towels.
3. Rub the fish with olive oil, then season with salt and pepper to taste.
4. Place the fish on the baking sheet and top with slices of lemon.
5. Bake for 10 to 12 minutes until the flesh flakes easily with a fork.
6. Meanwhile, combine the salsa ingredients in a bowl and chill until ready to serve.
7. Serve the fish hot with the mango salsa and extra lemon wedges.

Parmesan Stuffed Zucchini Boats

Ingredients:

2 medium zucchini
1 medium plum tomato, chopped
½ small red pepper, diced
½ small red onion, diced
¼ cup grated parmesan cheese
3 tbsp. ground almond meal
1 tsp. dried Italian seasoning
Salt and pepper to taste
Olive oil as needed

Directions:

1. Preheat the oven to 350°F.
2. Slice the zucchini in half lengthwise.
3. Use a sharp knife or spoon to hollow out the zucchini, reserving the flesh.
4. Brush the zucchini boats with olive oil and place them cut-side down on a baking sheet.
5. Bake for 5 to 8 minutes until tender.
6. Chop the zucchini flesh you removed and add it to a bowl with the remaining ingredients.
7. Spoon the mixture into the zucchini and place the boats back on the baking sheet.
8. Bake for 8 to 12 minutes until the filling is hot.

Roasted Garlic Pork Loin

Ingredients:

2 lbs. boneless pork loin
1 handful peeled garlic cloves
1 tbsp. olive oil
1 tbsp. dried rosemary
Salt and pepper to taste

Directions:

1. Preheat oven to 350°F.
2. Use a sharp knife to cut 1-inch slices into the pork on all sides.
3. Insert a clove of garlic into each cut.
4. Rub the skin of the pork with olive oil then sprinkle with rosemary, salt and pepper.
5. Place the pork loin upside down on a roasting pan and roast for 30 minutes.
6. Turn the pork loin fat-side up and roast for another 20 to 25 minutes until the internal temperature reaches 155°F.
7. Remove the pork loin to a cutting board and cover with foil.
8. Let stand for 10 minutes before carving.

Spicy Vegetable Curry

Ingredients:

3 tsp. olive oil, divided
1 yellow onion, diced
1 cup dry white rice
2 ¾ cups water, divided
1 tbsp. minced garlic
1 tsp. grated ginger
1 tbsp. red curry paste
1 cup canned coconut milk
1 large sweet potato, cubed
1 cup broccoli florets
1 cup cauliflower florets
1 cup baby carrots, halved

Directions:

1. Heat 1 tsp. olive oil in a saucepan over medium-high heat.
2. Stir in the ginger and onions and cook for 3 minutes.
3. Add the rice and 1 ½ cups water and stir well.
4. Bring the mixture to a boil then reduce heat and simmer until the rice is tender, about 15 minutes.
5. Remove from heat and let stand.
6. Heat the remaining oil in a heavy skillet over medium heat.
7. Add the garlic and onion and cook for 1 minute.
8. Stir in the curry paste, coconut milk and 1 cup water.
9. Bring to a boil.
10. Stir in the sweet potato, broccoli, cauliflower and carrot.
11. Season with salt and pepper to taste.

Flatten Your Wheat Belly

12. Reduce heat and simmer for 10 to 15 minutes, covered, until the vegetables are tender.
13. Serve the curry hot over the steamed rice.

The Wheat Belly Cookbook

Arugula Avocado Turkey Burgers

Ingredients:

1 lbs. lean ground turkey
1 large egg
2 tbsp. ground almond meal
1 tsp. dried parsley
Salt and pepper to taste
1 bunch fresh arugula, rinsed well
1 ripe avocado, pitted and sliced

Directions:

1. Preheat the broiler in your oven.
2. Arrange the arugula evenly on four plates and set aside.
3. Combine the turkey, egg, almond meal, parsley, salt and pepper in a mixing bowl.
4. Mix well by hand then shape into four even patties.
5. Place the patties on a broiler pan and broil for 4 to 5 minutes on each side until cooked through.
6. Place one turkey patty on each bed of arugula and top with avocado slices to serve.

Asian-Style Shrimp with Rice Noodles

Ingredients:

1 lbs. raw shrimp, peeled and deveined
1 tbsp. olive oil
1 tsp. minced garlic
1 tsp. minced ginger
8 oz. thin rice noodles
2 tbsp. soy sauce
2 tbsp. water
1 tbsp. hoisin sauce
1 tbsp. olive oil
1 tsp. dark sesame oil
½ tsp. crushed red pepper flakes

Directions:

1. Bring a pot of salted water to boil and cook the rice noodles according to the directions.
2. Drain the noodles and set aside.
3. Heat the oil in a skillet over medium-high heat.
4. Add the garlic and ginger and cook for 1 minute.
5. Stir in the shrimp and cook for 2 to 3 minutes, stirring often.
6. Add the rice noodles and stir well.
7. Whisk together the remaining ingredients and pour into the skillet.
8. Toss to coat and cook until heated through.

Roasted Red Pepper Zucchini Pasta

Ingredients:

1 tbsp. olive oil
1 tsp. minced garlic
1 medium yellow onion, diced
½ cup roasted red peppers in oil, chopped
2 large zucchini
¼ tsp. dried thyme
Salt and pepper to taste
2 tbsp. fresh chopped parsley

Directions:

1. Heat the olive oil in a skillet over medium heat.
2. Add the garlic and cook for 1 minute.
3. Stir in the onion and cook for 4 to 5 minutes until translucent.
4. Add the zucchini and toss with the dried thyme.
5. Cook for 2 minutes.
6. Add the roasted red pepper and stir well then cover.
7. Cook for 1 to 2 minutes until the zucchini is tender.
8. Season with salt and pepper to taste.
9. Serve hot, garnished with fresh parsley.

Herb Roasted Lamb Chops

Ingredients:

2 lbs. small bone-in lamb chops
1 tbsp. olive oil
1 tsp. dried rosemary
1 tsp. dried basil
1 tsp. dried oregano
Salt and pepper to taste

Directions:

1. Preheat the broiler in your oven.
2. Rub the lamb chops with olive oil and season with salt and pepper to taste.
3. Combine the spices in a small bowl.
4. Arrange the lamb chops on a broiler pan.
5. Sprinkle with the spice mixture then broil for 4 to 5 minutes on each side until cooked to the desired temperature.

Stewed Chicken with Peppers

Ingredients:

1 lbs. boneless skinless chicken, chopped
2 tbsp. olive oil
1 tbsp. minced garlic
2 sweet red peppers, sliced
1 green bell pepper, sliced
1 cup sliced mushrooms
1 cup chopped onions
1 cup diced tomato
1 cup organic chicken broth
2 bay leaves
1 tsp. dried oregano
Salt and pepper to taste

Directions:

1. Heat the oil in a deep skillet over medium-high heat.
2. Add the garlic and cook for 1 minute.
3. Stir in the onions and mushrooms and cook for about 5 minutes, stirring often.
4. Add the chicken and cook until lightly browned.
5. Stir in the remaining ingredients and bring to a simmer.
6. Reduce heat and simmer, covered, for 20 minutes or until the chicken is cooked through.
7. Season with salt and pepper to taste. Serve hot.

Seared Scallops with Rice Noodles

Ingredients:

1 lbs. large sea scallops, raw
8 oz. thin rice noodles
1 tbsp. olive oil
Salt and pepper to taste
1 to 2 tbsp. fresh chopped parsley

Directions:

1. Bring a pot of salted water to boil then add the rice noodles.
2. Remove from heat and let the rice noodles soak while you prepare the scallops
3. Rinse the scallops well and pat them dry with a paper towel.
4. Season the scallops with salt and pepper to taste.
5. Heat the oil in a heavy skillet over medium-high heat.
6. Add the scallops and cook for 2 to 3 minutes per side until browned and cooked through.
7. Drain the rice noodles and place them in a serving dish.
8. Drizzle with olive oil then season with salt and pepper to taste.
9. Serve the noodles topped with the scallops and sprinkle with parsley to garnish.

Side Dish Recipes

Rosemary Roasted Vegetables

Ingredients:

2 cups broccoli florets

2 cups cauliflower florets

2 medium Yukon gold potatoes, chopped

1 cup baby carrots

1 yellow onion, quartered

¼ cup organic vegetable broth

1 tbsp. dried rosemary

Salt and pepper to taste

Directions:

1. Preheat the oven to 400°F.
2. Combine the vegetables in a glass baking dish.
3. Drizzle with vegetable broth and sprinkle with rosemary, salt and pepper.
4. Roast the vegetables for 30 minutes then turn with a slotted spoon.
5. Let the vegetables roast for another 20 to 25 minutes until tender.

Red Potatoes and Green Beans

Ingredients:

1 tbsp. olive oil
1 tsp. minced garlic
1 small shallot, diced
2 cups diced red potato
1 lbs. green beans, trimmed
¼ cup water
1 medium tomato, diced
Salt and pepper to taste

Directions:

1. Heat the oil in a skillet over medium-high heat.
2. Add the garlic and shallot and cook for 1 minute.
3. Stir in the potato and green beans and cook for 1 minute more.
4. Add the water then cover and cook for 5 minutes until the beans are tender.
5. Remove the lid then stir in the tomatoes, salt and pepper.
6. Cook for 3 to 5 minutes more until the potatoes are tender. Serve hot.

Parmesan Grilled Asparagus

Ingredients:

1 bunch fresh asparagus spears, ends trimmed
¼ cup shaved parmesan cheese
2 tbsp. olive oil
Salt and pepper to taste

Directions:

1. Preheat your grill to medium-high heat.
2. Toss the asparagus with the olive oil and season with salt and pepper to taste.
3. Arrange the spears on the grill and cook for 4 to 5 minutes, turning every minute or so, until the asparagus is tender.
4. Transfer the asparagus to a dish and toss with the shaved parmesan cheese to serve.

The Wheat Belly Cookbook

Creamy Potato Salad

Ingredients:

1 lbs. fingerling potatoes, chopped
1 hardboiled egg, peeled and chopped
2 tbsp. olive oil mayonnaise
1 tsp. Dijon mustard
¼ cup diced celery
2 tbsp. diced red onion
Pinch salt and pepper

Directions:

1. Fill a saucepan with water and add the fingerling potatoes.
2. Bring to a boil then reduce heat to medium-high, cover, and cook for 5 minutes.
3. Drain the potatoes and place them in a bowl.
4. Add the remaining ingredients and toss well to combine.
5. Serve warm or chill until ready to serve.

Pineapple Carrot Coleslaw

Ingredients:

10 oz. matchstick carrots
1 cup fresh chopped pineapple
1 green onion, sliced thin
½ cup golden raisins
2 tbsp. canola oil
2 tbsp. fresh lemon juice
2 tbsp. pineapple juice
1 tbsp. honey
Pinch salt and pepper

Directions:

1. Whisk together the oil, lemon juice, honey, pineapple juice, salt and pepper in a small bowl.
2. Combine the remaining ingredients in a serving bowl and toss with the dressing.
3. Chill until ready to serve

The Wheat Belly Cookbook

Balsamic-Marinated Cucumber Salad

Ingredients:

4 cups cucumber, thinly sliced
2 tbsp. olive oil
1 tbsp. balsamic vinegar
1 tbsp. red wine vinegar
1 tbsp. honey
1 tbsp. toasted sesame seeds
Pinch salt and pepper

Directions:

1. Whisk together all the ingredients aside from the cucumber.
2. Place the cucumber in a bowl and add the dressing.
3. Toss well to coat, then chill until ready to serve.

Grilled Zucchini

Ingredients:

2 large zucchini
2 tbsp. olive oil
1 tbsp. balsamic vinegar
Salt and pepper to taste

Directions:

1. Preheat the grill to medium-high heat and line the grates with foil.
2. Slice the zucchini into ¼-inch slices and brush with olive oil and balsamic vinegar.
3. Season the zucchini with salt and pepper to taste then arrange the slices on the grill.
4. Cook for 2 to 3 minutes on each side until tender and slightly charred.
5. Transfer to a bowl to serve.

Heirloom Tomato Mozzarella Salad

Ingredients:

1 large heirloom tomato, chopped
1 cup cherry tomatoes, halved
1 cup balled fresh mozzarella, halved
2 tbsp. fresh basil, minced
1 tbsp. fresh lemon juice
1 tbsp. balsamic vinegar
Pinch salt and pepper

Directions:

1. Combine the tomatoes and mozzarella in a serving bowl.
2. Toss the mixture with the lemon juice, balsamic vinegar and basil.
3. Season with salt and pepper to taste.
4. Chill until ready to serve.

Garlic Mashed Potatoes

Ingredients:

1 lbs. Yukon gold potatoes
¼ cup skim or 1% milk
2 tbsp. softened butter
1 tbsp. minced garlic
Salt and pepper to taste

Directions:

1. Peel the potatoes and cut them into 1-inch chunks.
2. Place the potatoes in a pot of salted water and bring to a boil.
3. Boil the potatoes, covered, for 6 to 8 minutes until fork tender.
4. Drain the potatoes and place them back in the pot.
5. Mash the potatoes with a potato masher and stir in the remaining ingredients. Serve hot.

The Wheat Belly Cookbook

Honeyed Bacon Brussels Sprouts

Ingredients:

1 tsp. olive oil
1 lbs. small Brussels sprouts
4 slices uncooked bacon
1 tbsp. honey
Salt and pepper to taste
Water as needed

Directions:

1. Trim the ends from the Brussels sprouts and cut each one in half.
2. Heat the oil in a skillet over medium-high heat.
3. Add the Brussels sprouts and toss to coat with oil.
4. Add 1 to 2 tbsp. water then quickly cover the skillet.
5. Steam the Brussels sprouts for 3 to 4 minutes until they turn bright green.
6. Spoon the Brussels sprouts into a bowl and cover.
7. Chop the bacon and add it to the skillet.
8. Cook for 3 to 4 minutes until the bacon is crisp then add the steamed Brussels sprouts.
9. Toss to coat, then stir in the honey and season with salt and pepper to taste.
10. Simmer for 3 to 4 minutes then serve hot.

Grilled Vegetable Skewers

Ingredients:

1 large yellow onion, cut into 2-inch chunks
10 whole mushrooms, cut in half
1 sweet red pepper, cut into 2-inch chunks
1 green bell pepper, cut into 2-inch chunks
1 to 2 tbsp. olive oil
Salt and pepper to taste

Directions:

1. Preheat your grill to medium-high heat and line the grates with aluminum foil.
2. Slide the sliced vegetables onto metal skewers and brush them with olive oil.
3. Season the vegetables with salt and pepper to taste then arrange them on the grill.
4. Cook for 2 to 3 minutes on each side, turning often, until the vegetables are tender and lightly charred.
5. Slide the vegetables off the skewers to serve.

Sautéed Swiss Chard with Lemon

Ingredients:

1 bunch fresh Swiss chard
2 tbsp. water
1 tbsp. olive oil
2 tsp. minced garlic
2 tsp. fresh lemon juice
Salt and pepper to taste

Directions:

1. Rinse the Swiss chard well and coarsely chop the leaves.
2. Heat the olive oil in a skillet and add the garlic.
3. Cook for one minute then stir in the Swiss chard and water.
4. Let the greens cook for 3 to 4 minutes until they begin to soften.
5. Stir in the lemon juice and season with salt and pepper to taste. Serve hot.

Snack and Beverage Recipes

The Wheat Belly Cookbook

Mini Oatmeal Muffins

Ingredients:

2 cups old-fashioned oats
¼ cup packed brown sugar
1 ½ tsp. ground cinnamon
1 tsp. baking powder
Pinch of salt
1 ½ cups skim milk
¼ cup unsweetened applesauce
½ cup liquid egg whites
½ cup raisins

Directions:

1. Preheat the oven to 350°F and grease a mini cupcake pan with cooking spray.
2. Combine the oats, brown sugar, baking powder, cinnamon and salt in a mixing bowl and stir well.
3. In another bowl, whisk together the milk, applesauce and egg whites.
4. Whisk the liquid ingredients into the oat mixture then fold in the raisins.
5. Spoon the batter into the prepared cupcake pan, filling each cup.
6. Bake for 25 to 35 minutes until a knife inserted in the center comes out clean.
7. Cool in the pan for 5 minutes, then turn out onto a wire rack to cool completely.

Strawberry Yogurt Parfaits

Ingredients:

1 cup plain nonfat Greek yogurt
1 cup sliced strawberries
¼ cup gluten-free granola

Directions:

1. Spoon about ¼ cup yogurt into the bottom of each of two parfait glasses.
2. Top the yogurt with about 1/3 cup sliced strawberries.
3. Spoon the remaining yogurt on top of the strawberries and top with the remaining strawberries.
4. Sprinkle with granola to serve.

Lemon Garlic Hummus

Ingredients:

1 head garlic, unpeeled
1 (19 oz.) can chickpeas, drained
2 tbsp. fresh lemon juice
2 tbsp. water
1 tbsp. tahini
1 tbsp. fresh chopped parsley
Salt and pepper to taste

Directions:

1. Preheat the oven to 400°F and slice the top off an unpeeled head of garlic.
2. Drizzle the garlic with extra oil then wrap in aluminum foil.
3. Roast the garlic for about 35 minutes until tender then unwrap and let sit until cool enough to handle.
4. Squeeze the garlic cloves into a blender.
5. Add the remaining ingredients and blend until smooth and well combined.
6. Serve with chips or chopped veggies.

Avocado Deviled Eggs

Ingredients:

10 hardboiled eggs, peeled
1 ripe avocado, pitted
¼ cup olive oil mayonnaise
½ tbsp. fresh lemon juice
Salt and pepper to taste

Directions:

1. Carefully cut the eggs in half lengthwise and scoop the yolks into a bowl.
2. Arrange the eggs on a platter and set aside.
3. Mash the egg yolks with a fork then blend in the avocado, mayonnaise, lemon juice, salt and pepper.
4. Blend until smooth then spoon the mixture back into the eggs and chill until ready to serve.

Toasted Nut Trail Mix

Ingredients:

1 lbs. raw almonds
1 cup halved walnuts
1 cup raw shelled peanuts
2 tbsp. olive oil
Sea salt to taste

Directions:

1. Preheat the oven to 350°F and line a baking sheet with parchment paper.
2. Combine the nuts in a mixing bowl with the olive oil and sea salt.
3. Toss well and spread in a single layer on the baking sheet.
4. Bake the nuts for 10 to 12 minutes, stirring once, until lightly browned.
5. Allow the nuts to cool then store in an airtight container.

Sesame Kale Chips

Ingredients:

1 bunch fresh kale
2 tbsp. olive oil
1 tbsp. sesame seeds
Pinch salt

Directions:

1. Preheat oven to 350°F and line a baking sheet with parchment.
2. Rinse the kale well and trim the ends.
3. Dry the leaves on a paper towel and tear them into bite-sized pieces by hand.
4. Place the kale in a large bowl and toss with olive oil, sesame seeds and salt.
5. Arrange the leaves in a single layer on the baking sheet and bake for 15 to 20 minutes until crisp.

Yogurt-Covered Bananas

Ingredients:

2 ripe bananas, peeled
1 cup plain nonfat yogurt

Directions:

1. Slice the bananas into ½-inch slices.
2. Cover a plate with plastic wrap and set it aside.
3. Use a fork or metal skewer to dip each slice in yogurt then arrange them on the plate in a single layer.
4. Freeze the bananas until the yogurt is solid then enjoy.

Sweet Potato Fries

Ingredients:

2 large sweet potatoes, peeled
2 tbsp. olive oil
1 tbsp. light brown sugar
½ tsp. chili powder
Salt and pepper to taste

Directions:

1. Preheat oven to 450°F and line a baking sheet with parchment.
2. Combine the brown sugar, chili powder, salt and pepper in a small bowl.
3. Slice the sweet potatoes into ½-inch thick sticks and place them in a large bowl.
4. Drizzle with oil and toss to coat.
5. Add the brown sugar mixture and toss well.
6. Spread the sweet potatoes in a single layer on the baking sheet and bake for 15 minutes.
7. Carefully flip the fries then bake for another 5 to 10 minutes until lightly browned.

Dried Fruit and Nut Trail Mix

Ingredients:

1 cup whole cashews
½ cup dry-roasted peanuts
¼ cup toasted almonds
¼ cup shelled pistachios
½ cup raisins
¼ cup dried cranberries
¼ cup dried cherries, chopped
Salt and pepper to taste

Directions:

1. Combine all of the ingredients in a bowl and toss with salt and pepper to season.
2. Store in an airtight container.

Roasted Red Pepper Hummus

Ingredients:

1 (15 oz.) can chickpeas, drained
¾ cup roasted red peppers, chopped
¼ cup tahini
2 tbsp. fresh lemon juice
2 tbsp. olive oil
1 clove garlic, minced
Pinch salt and pepper

Directions:

1. Combine the tahini and lemon juice in a food processer and blend for 30 seconds.
2. Add the garlic and salt and blend 10 seconds more.
3. Add the remaining ingredients and blend until smooth and well combined.
4. Serve with chips or chopped veggies.

The Wheat Belly Cookbook

Honey Almond Milk

Ingredients:

1 cup raw almonds
2 cups water
2 tsp. honey

Directions:

1. Soak the almonds in water overnight then drain well.
2. Place the almonds in a blender with the water and blend on high speed for 2 minutes.
3. Strain the liquid through cheesecloth and discard the solids.
4. Whisk in the honey and refrigerate until ready to serve.

Cinnamon Pumpkin Latte

Ingredients:

2 cups 1% milk
½ cup brewed coffee, hot
2 tbsp. pumpkin puree
1 ½ tbsp. brown sugar
1 tbsp. vanilla extract
½ tsp. pumpkin pie spice

Directions:

1. Whisk together the milk, pumpkin and sugar in a small saucepan over medium heat.
2. Remove from heat then whisk in the remaining ingredients.
3. Pour into mugs and garnish with whipped cream, if desired, to serve.

The Wheat Belly Cookbook

Peppermint Hot Chocolate

Ingredients:

4 cups 1% milk
½ cup white sugar
¼ cup unsweetened cocoa powder
1/3 cup boiling water
1 tsp. peppermint extract

Directions:

1. Whisk together the water, sugar and cocoa powder in a medium saucepan.
2. Bring the mixture to a boil then whisk in the milk – do not let the milk boil.
3. Remove from the heat and whisk in the peppermint extract.
4. Pour into mugs to serve.

Strawberry Kiwi Smoothie

Ingredients:

2 cups frozen sliced strawberries
2 ripe kiwi, peeled and sliced
½ cup organic apple juice
½ cup plain nonfat Greek yogurt
½ cup ice cubes

Directions:

1. Combine all of the ingredients in a blender.
2. Blend the mixture until smooth, adding more ice if desired to thicken.
3. Divide between two glasses and serve immediately.

Pineapple Kale Smoothie

Ingredients:

2 cups frozen pineapple chunks
1 cup chopped kale leaves
1 cup unsweetened coconut milk
½ cup organic apple juice
½ cup plain nonfat Greek yogurt

Directions:

1. Combine all of the ingredients in a blender.
2. Blend the mixture until smooth, adding more ice if desired to thicken.
3. Divide between two glasses and serve immediately.

Groovy Garden Green Smoothie

Ingredients:

2 large leaves romaine lettuce, chopped
2 leaves curly kale, chopped
½ cup chopped mustard greens
1 cup unsweetened almond milk
½ cup plain nonfat Greek yogurt
1 tsp. honey

Directions:

1. Combine all of the ingredients in a blender.
2. Blend the mixture until smooth, adding more ice if desired to thicken.
3. Divide between two glasses and serve immediately.

The Wheat Belly Cookbook

Broccoli Blueberry Smoothie

Ingredients:

2 cups frozen blueberries
1 cup fresh chopped broccoli
1 cup organic apple juice
½ cup plain nonfat Greek yogurt
1 tbsp. honey

Directions:

1. Combine all of the ingredients in a blender.
2. Blend the mixture until smooth, adding more ice if desired to thicken.
3. Divide between two glasses and serve immediately.

Savory Tomato Basil Smoothie

Ingredients:

2 small plum tomatoes
2 to 3 fresh basil leaves
1 large leaf kale, chopped
1 cup organic apple juice
½ cup plain nonfat Greek yogurt
½ cup ice cubes

Directions:

1. Combine all of the ingredients in a blender.
2. Blend the mixture until smooth, adding more ice if desired to thicken.
3. Divide between two glasses and serve immediately.

Condiment Recipes

Homemade Ketchup

Ingredients:

1 (14.5 oz.) can diced tomatoes, drained
¼ cup diced yellow onion
3 tbsp. red wine vinegar
2 tbsp. dark brown sugar
1 clove garlic, minced
1 ½ tsp. olive oil
½ tsp. salt
¼ tsp. black pepper
Pinch of allspice, ginger and cayenne

Directions:

1. Heat the olive oil in a skillet over medium heat.
2. Stir in the garlic and onion and cook for 3 minutes.
3. Add the remaining ingredients and simmer for about 20 minutes until the tomatoes are tender.
4. Blend the mixture in a blender until smooth then strain through a mesh sieve.
5. Return to heat and cook over medium-low heat for 10 to 20 minutes until slightly thickened.
6. Cool to room temperature then store in the refrigerator.

The Wheat Belly Cookbook

Spicy Mustard

Ingredients:

¼ cup dry mustard seeds
¼ cup white wine vinegar
¼ cup water
2 tsp. maple syrup
½ tsp. ground turmeric
Pinch salt and pepper

Directions:

1. Blend all of the ingredients in a small metal bowl.
2. Cover and let stand for 48 hours.
3. Pour the mixture into a blender and blend until smooth.
4. Add more water, if desired, to thin the mustard.

Basil Pine Nut Pesto

Ingredients:

2 cups fresh basil leaves
½ cup grated parmesan cheese
½ cup olive oil
¼ cup toasted pine nuts
2 large cloves garlic, minced
Pinch salt and pepper

Directions:

1. Place the basil leaves and pine nuts in a food processor and pulse several times to chop.
2. Add the parmesan cheese and garlic and pulse the mixture a few more times.
3. With the food processor running, drizzle in the olive oil.
4. Season with salt and pepper to serve.

Fresh Tomato Salsa

Ingredients:

1 lbs. plum tomatoes, diced
1 small jalapeno, seeded and minced (optional)
½ small green pepper, diced
½ small red pepper, diced
½ bunch fresh cilantro, chopped
1 tsp. salt
¼ tsp. ground cumin

Directions:

1. Combine all of the ingredients in a mixing bowl.
2. Toss well to combine then cover and refrigerate for several hours before serving.

Olive Tapenade

Ingredients:

1 cup pitted black olives
1 cup pitted green olives
¼ cup sundried tomatoes in oil, chopped
¼ cup olive oil
1 tbsp. capers
1 tsp. minced garlic
½ tsp. dried basil
½ tsp. dried parsley
½ tsp. dried oregano
Pinch salt and pepper

Directions:

1. Place all of the ingredients, aside from the olive oil, in a food processor.
2. Pulse several times until coarsely chopped.
3. Drizzle in the oil while pulsing the mixture then store in the refrigerator.

The Wheat Belly Cookbook

Red Wine Vinaigrette

Ingredients:

½ cup olive oil
2 tbsp. red wine vinegar
1 ½ tsp. Dijon mustard
½ tsp. dried basil
½ tsp. dried oregano
Pinch salt and pepper

Directions:

1. Combine the vinegar, mustard and spices in a small bowl.
2. Mix well, then drizzle in the oil while whisking.
3. Store in the refrigerator.

Roasted Garlic Dressing

Ingredients:

1 head garlic
½ cup olive oil
2 tbsp. white wine vinegar
2 tbsp. grated parmesan cheese
1 ½ tsp. Dijon mustard
1 tsp. dried basil
Pinch salt and pepper

Directions:

7. Preheat the oven to 400°F and slice the top off an unpeeled head of garlic.
8. Drizzle the garlic with extra oil then wrap in aluminum foil.
9. Roast the garlic for about 35 minutes until tender then unwrap and let sit until cool enough to handle.
10. Squeeze the garlic cloves into a blender.
11. Add the remaining ingredients and pulse until finely blended.
12. Store in the refrigerator.

The Wheat Belly Cookbook

Mediterranean Feta Dressing

Ingredients:

½ cup olive oil
½ cup crumbled feta cheese
2 tbsp. red wine vinegar
1 tsp. Dijon mustard
1 small diced tomato
1 tsp. dried parsley
½ tsp. dried basil
½ tsp. dried oregano
Pinch salt and pepper

Directions:

1. Combine the vinegar, mustard, spices, salt and pepper in a small bowl.
2. Mix well then drizzle in the oil while whisking.
3. Whisk in the remaining ingredients then store in the refrigerator to chill before serving.

White Wine Vinaigrette

Ingredients:

½ cup olive oil
2 tbsp. white wine vinegar
1 ½ tsp. Dijon mustard
1 small minced shallot
½ tsp. dried basil
½ tsp. dried oregano
Pinch salt and pepper

Directions:

4. Combine the vinegar, mustard, shallot and spices in a small bowl.
5. Mix well then drizzle in the oil while whisking.
6. Store in the refrigerator to chill before serving.

The Wheat Belly Cookbook

Honey Mustard Dressing

Ingredients:

¼ cup olive oil
¼ cup canola oil
2 tbsp. fresh lime juice
2 tsp. honey
2 tsp. Dijon mustard
¼ tsp. dried thyme
Pinch salt and pepper

Directions:

1. Combine the lime juice, honey, Dijon mustard, thyme, salt and pepper to in a bowl.
2. Mix well then drizzle in the oils while whisking.
3. Store in the refrigerator to chill before serving.

Easy Italian Dressing

Ingredients:

½ cup olive oil
2 tbsp. red wine vinegar
2 tbsp. minced red onion
2 tbsp. fresh chopped parsley
1 tbsp. fresh chopped basil
1 tsp. dried oregano
1 clove garlic, minced
Pinch salt and pepper

Directions:

1. Combine the onion, parsley, basil, oregano, garlic, salt and pepper in a small bowl.
2. Use a fork to mash the mixture into a paste.
3. Whisk in the red wine vinegar then drizzle in the oil while whisking.
4. Store in the refrigerator to chill before serving.

The Wheat Belly Cookbook

Creamy Buttermilk Dressing

Ingredients:

½ cup nonfat buttermilk, chilled
2 tbsp. raspberry-flavored vinegar
1 tbsp. fresh chopped basil
1 tbsp. fresh chopped dill
1 tsp. fresh chopped chives
½ tsp. minced garlic
Pinch salt and pepper

Directions:

1. Whisk together the buttermilk and vinegar in a small mixing bowl.
2. Add the remaining ingredients and blend well.
3. Store in a glass jar in the refrigerator to chill before using.

Cilantro Herb Dressing

Ingredients:

1 cup grape seed oil
1 cup sliced green onion
¼ cup white wine vinegar
2 tbsp. fresh lemon juice
2 tbsp. fresh lime juice
½ cup chopped cilantro
Pinch salt and pepper

Directions:

1. Combine all of the ingredients in a blender.
2. Blend the mixture until smooth and store in the refrigerator until ready to use.

Dessert Recipes

Blueberry Mint Sorbet

Ingredients:

1 ½ cups fresh blueberries
¾ cup water
¼ cup chopped mint leaves
2 tbsp. honey
1 tbsp. fresh lemon juice

Directions:

1. Combine the water, honey and lemon juice in a small saucepan over medium heat.
2. Stir the mixture until the honey melts.
3. Add the blueberries and mint leaves then cook for 5 to 7 minutes until steaming.
4. Remove from heat and strain the mixture through a mesh sieve. Discard the solids.
5. Pour the liquid into a shallow dish and freeze until solid.
6. Just before serving, break into pieces and blend in a food processor until smooth.

Chocolate Mocha Frozen Yogurt

Ingredients:

1 (12 oz.) can evaporated milk
1 cup plain nonfat Greek yogurt
¾ cup superfine sugar
½ cup semisweet chocolate chips
¼ cup brewed coffee, cooled
2 tsp. cornstarch
1 tsp. vanilla extract

Directions:

1. Whisk together the evaporated milk, sugar and chocolate chips in a small saucepan over medium-low heat.
2. Heat until the chocolate is melted and whisk smooth.
3. Remove from heat and whisk in the cornstarch and vanilla extract.
4. Let sit until thickened.
5. Whisk in the yogurt and coffee until smooth.
6. Pour the mixture into a freezer-safe plastic container.
7. Cover and freeze for 1 hour. Stir then freeze the mixture until solid.
8. Remove the frozen yogurt from the freezer 15 minutes before serving to thaw.

Honey Baked Apples

Ingredients:

4 ripe apples
1 cup organic apple juice
½ cup raisins
2 tbsp. honey
2 tbsp. light brown sugar

Directions:

1. Preheat oven to 350°F.
2. Slice the tops off the apples and set them aside.
3. Using a sharp knife, remove the core from the apples.
4. Combine the remaining ingredients, excluding the apple juice, in a small bowl then stuff the mixture into the four apples and replace the tops.
5. Arrange the apples in a small baking dish and pour the apple juice into the dish around the apples.
6. Bake for 15 to 18 minutes until the apples are tender.

The Wheat Belly Cookbook

Coconut Flour Brownies

Ingredients:

1 cup honey or maple syrup
½ cup unsweetened cocoa powder
½ cup coconut flour
1/3 cup coconut oil
6 large eggs, whisked
1 tsp. vanilla extract
Pinch salt
½ cup mini chocolate chips

Directions:

1. Preheat oven to 350°F and lightly grease a square glass baking dish.
2. Combine the coconut oil and cocoa powder in a small saucepan over medium heat.
3. Heat the mixture until the coconut oil is melted, then stir until smooth and fully combined.
4. In a mixing bowl, beat together the eggs, honey and vanilla extract.
5. Beat in the coconut oil/cocoa powder mixture.
6. Add the coconut flour and salt and beat until smooth.
7. Fold in the chocolate chips.
8. Pour the batter into the prepared dish and spread evenly.
9. Bake for 30 to 35 minutes until a knife inserted in the center comes out clean.
10. Cool completely before cutting to serve.

Cinnamon Baked Bananas

Ingredients:

2 ripe bananas, peeled
1 tbsp. honey
Ground cinnamon to taste

Directions:

1. Preheat the oven to 350°F and lightly grease a small casserole dish.
2. Slice the bananas to the desired thickness and arrange them in the dish.
3. Drizzle with honey and sprinkle with cinnamon.
4. Bake for 10 to 12 minutes until tender then spoon into bowls to serve.

The Wheat Belly Cookbook

Almond Flour Chocolate Chip Cookies

Ingredients:

2 ½ cups almond flour
½ cup canola oil
½ cup honey
3 large eggs, whisked
1 tsp. baking soda
1 tsp. vanilla extract
Pinch of salt
1 cup semi-sweet chocolate chips

Directions:

1. Preheat the oven to 375°F and line baking sheets with parchment.
2. Combine the flour, baking soda and salt in a mixing bowl.
3. In a separate bowl, beat together the canola oil, honey, eggs and vanilla extract.
4. Add the dry ingredients to the wet and beat until smooth.
5. Fold in the chocolate chips.
6. Drop the batter in tablespoons onto the prepared baking sheets.
7. Bake for 8 to 12 minutes until just golden around the edges.
8. Cool in the pans for 5 minutes then transfer to a cooling rack to finish cooling.

Pecan-Crust Pumpkin Pie

Ingredients:

1 cup chopped pecans
2 tbsp. butter, melted
2 tbsp. white sugar

1 (15 oz.) can pumpkin puree
1 (12 oz.) can evaporated milk
¾ cup white sugar
2 large eggs, whisked
1 ½ tsp. pumpkin pie spice
Pinch salt

Directions:

1. Preheat the oven to 425°F.
2. Place the pecans in a food processor and pulse until finely chopped.
3. Add the butter and sugar and pulse to combine.
4. Press the mixture into a pie pan and spread evenly along the bottom and sides.
5. In a mixing bowl, combine the sugar, pumpkin pie spice and salt.
6. Add the beaten eggs and pumpkin and beat until smooth.
7. Slowly pour in the evaporated milk and stir until combined.
8. Pour the mixture into the prepared pie crust.

The Wheat Belly Cookbook

9. Bake for 15 minutes then reduce heat to 350°F and bake for another 40 to 50 minutes until the center is set.

10. Cool for at least 2 hours before serving.

Lemon Lime Sorbet

Ingredients:

¾ cup water
¼ cup fresh lemon juice
3 tbsp. fresh lime juice
2 tbsp. honey

Directions:

1. Combine the water, honey and lemon juice in a small saucepan over medium heat.
2. Stir the mixture until the honey melts.
3. Remove from heat and whisk in the lemon and lime juice.
4. Strain the mixture through a mesh sieve.
5. Pour the liquid into a shallow dish and freeze until solid.
6. Just before serving, break into pieces and blend in a food processor until smooth.

The Wheat Belly Cookbook

Chocolate Coconut Brownies

Ingredients:

1 cup honey

½ cup unsweetened cocoa powder

½ cup coconut flour

1/3 cup coconut oil

6 large eggs, whisked

1 tsp. vanilla extract

Pinch salt

½ cup mini chocolate chips

½ cup unsweetened flaked coconut

Directions:

1. Preheat oven to 350°F and lightly grease a square glass baking dish.
2. Combine the coconut oil and cocoa powder in a small saucepan over medium heat.
3. Heat the mixture until the coconut oil is melted, then stir until smooth and combined.
4. In a mixing bowl, beat together the eggs, honey and vanilla extract.
5. Beat in the coconut oil/cocoa powder mixture.
6. Add the coconut flour and salt and beat until smooth.
7. Fold in the chocolate chips and flaked coconut
8. Pour the batter into the prepared dish and spread evenly.
9. Bake for 30 to 35 minutes until a knife inserted in the center comes out clean.
10. Cool completely before cutting to serve.

Easy Vanilla Cupcakes

Ingredients:

½ cup coconut flour
½ cup honey
½ cup coconut oil, melted
6 large eggs, beaten
1 tsp. vanilla extract
¼ tsp. baking soda
Pinch salt

Directions:

1. Preheat oven to 350°F and line a cupcake pan with paper liners.
2. Combine the coconut flour, baking soda and salt in a mixing bowl.
3. In another bowl, beat tighter the honey, coconut oil, eggs and vanilla extract.
4. Add the dry ingredients to the wet and beat until smooth.
5. Spoon the batter into the cupcake pan, filling each cup about 2/3 full.
6. Bake for 20 minutes until a knife inserted in the center comes out clean.

The Wheat Belly Cookbook

Raspberry Thumbprint Cookies

Ingredients:

1 pouch gluten-free sugar cookie mix
2 tbsp. almond flour
½ cup softened butter
1 large egg, whisked
1/3 cup raspberry jam

Directions:

1. Preheat oven to 375°F and line a baking sheet with parchment.
2. Combine the sugar cookie mix, almond flour and butter in a mixing bowl.
3. Add the egg and mix until combined.
4. Roll the dough into 1-inch balls and arrange them on the baking sheet.
5. Using your thumb, make an indentation in the center of each cookie.
6. Spoon about ¼ teaspoon raspberry jam into each indentation.
7. Bake for 8 to 10 minutes until the edges are golden brown.
8. Cool on the pan for 5 minutes then remove to a wire rack to finish cooling.

Chocolate-Covered Strawberries

Ingredients:

12 whole strawberries, stems removed
1 cup semisweet chocolate chips
1 tsp. vegetable shortening

Directions:

1. Line a baking sheet with parchment paper and set it aside.
2. Rinse the strawberries well and pat them dry with a paper towel.
3. Place the chocolate chips in a microwave-safe dish and heat on high at 20 second intervals, stirring after each.
4. Heat the chocolate chips until they are fully melted then stir until smooth.
5. Stir the shortening into the melted chocolate to thin it.
6. Dip the strawberries into the chocolate by hand then set them on the baking sheet.
7. Place the baking sheet in the refrigerator until the chocolate is solid.

The Wheat Belly Cookbook

Maple Cherry Cookies

Ingredients:

2 ½ cups almond flour
½ cup canola oil
½ cup maple syrup
3 large eggs, whisked
1 tsp. baking soda
1 tsp. almond extract
Pinch of salt
1 cup dried cherries, chopped

Directions:

1. Preheat the oven to 375°F and line baking sheets with parchment.
2. Combine the flour, baking soda and salt in a mixing bowl.
3. In a separate bowl, beat together the canola oil, maple syrup, eggs and almond extract.
4. Add the dry ingredients to the wet and beat until smooth.
5. Fold in the chopped dried cherries.
6. Drop the batter in tablespoons onto the prepared baking sheets.
7. Bake for 8 to 12 minutes until just golden around the edges.
8. Cool in the pans for 5 minutes then transfer to a cooling rack to finish cooling.

Cherry Chip Frozen Yogurt

Ingredients:

3 cups plain nonfat Greek yogurt
¾ cup superfine sugar
1 tsp. vanilla extract
½ cup mini chocolate chips
½ cup chopped dried cherries

Directions:

1. Whisk together the yogurt, sugar and vanilla extract until smooth.
2. Add the chocolate chips and dried cherries and stir well.
3. Pour the mixture into a freezer-safe plastic container.
4. Cover and freeze for 1 hour. Stir then freeze the mixture until solid.
5. Remove the frozen yogurt from the freezer 15 minutes before serving to thaw.

The Wheat Belly Cookbook

Peppermint Chocolate Bark

Ingredients:

2 cups semisweet chocolate chips
1 ½ cups peppermint candies, crushed

Directions:

1. Line a rimmed baking sheet with foil.
2. Melt the chocolate chips in a double boiler over medium-low heat and stir until smooth.
3. Pour the melted chocolate into the baking sheet and spread evenly.
4. Sprinkled the crushed peppermint candies over the chocolate.
5. Refrigerate the chocolate until set.
6. Remove the bark from the foil and break into large chunks by hand.

Chocolate Coconut Cupcakes

Ingredients:

½ cup honey or maple syrup
¼ cup coconut flour
¼ cup unsweetened cocoa powder
¼ cup coconut oil, melted
¼ cup unsweetened flaked coconut
3 large eggs, whisked
½ tsp. baking soda
½ tsp. coconut extract
Pinch salt

Directions:

1. Preheat oven to 350°F and line a cupcake pan with paper liners.
2. Combine the coconut flour, cocoa powder, baking soda and salt in a mixing bowl.
3. In another bowl, beat together the honey, coconut oil, eggs and coconut extract.
4. Add the dry ingredients to the wet and beat until smooth.
5. Fold in the flaked coconut
6. Spoon the batter into the cupcake pan, filling each cup about 2/3 full.
7. Bake for 20 minutes, until a knife inserted in the center comes out clean.

The Wheat Belly Cookbook

Chocolate Almond Bark

Ingredients:

2 cups semisweet chocolate chips
1 ½ cups chopped almonds

Directions:

1. Line a rimmed baking sheet with foil.
2. Melt the chocolate chips in a double boiler over medium-low heat and stir until smooth.
3. Pour the melted chocolate into the baking sheet and spread evenly.
4. Sprinkled the chopped almonds over the chocolate.
5. Refrigerate the chocolate until set.
6. Remove the bark from the foil and break into large chunks by hand.

Frozen Chocolate Covered Bananas

Ingredients:

4 large bananas, ripe
¾ cup chocolate chips
¼ cup crushed peanuts

Directions:

1. Peel the bananas and cut each one in half.
2. Melt the chocolate chips in a double boiler over medium-low heat and stir until smooth.
3. Dip the bananas in the melted chocolate and place them on a parchment-lined baking sheet.
4. Sprinkle with peanuts then refrigerate until the chocolate is solid.

Conclusion

After reading this book, you should have a good idea why wheat is bad for your health and what you can do to eliminate it from your diet. Eliminating wheat may involve eliminating some of your favorite foods – like bread and pasta – but you will soon learn that there are plenty of healthier alternatives.

Use the recipes in this book to kick-start your wheat belly diet and have fun taste-testing everything! Before you will be living without wheat and loving it.

Enjoy this book and good luck to you as you get started on your way road to good health and well-being!